THE DREAM THEY SHARED

by Myka-Lynne Sokoloff
illustrated by Bruce Emmett

SCHOOL PUBLISHERS

Copyright © by Harcourt, Inc.

All rights reserved. No part of this publication may be reproduced or transmitted in any form or by any means, electronic or mechanical, including photocopy, recording, or any information storage and retrieval system, without permission in writing from the publisher.

Requests for permission to make copies of any part of the work should be addressed to School Permissions and Copyrights, Harcourt, Inc., 6277 Sea Harbor Drive, Orlando, Florida 32887–6777. Fax: 407-345-2418.

HARCOURT and the Harcourt Logo are trademarks of Harcourt, Inc., registered in the United States of America and/or other jurisdictions.

Printed in Mexico

ISBN 10: 0-15-350279-7
ISBN 13: 978-0-15-350279-8

Ordering Options
ISBN 10: 0-15-349940-0 (Grade 5 ELL Collection)
ISBN 13: 978-0-15-349940-1 (Grade 5 ELL Collection)
ISBN 10: 0-15-357314-7 (package of 5)
ISBN 13: 978-0-15-357314-9 (package of 5)

If you have received these materials as examination copies free of charge, Harcourt School Publishers retains title to the materials and they may not be resold. Resale of examination copies is strictly prohibited and is illegal.

Possession of this publication in print format does not entitle users to convert this publication, or any portion of it, into electronic format.

2 3 4 5 6 7 8 9 10   126   12 11 10 09 08 07

From the Notebooks of Leonardo da Vinci

1476
Florence, Italy

I have my own studio at last. Now I can paint a picture by myself, from beginning to end. I learned much in the workshop of Verrocchio. My teacher is a fine painter. He also taught me to make statues. Still, I am pleased to work alone. I can choose what I want to paint.

I can work on anything I please. Other artists just make art. They paint pictures or they make statues. I cannot limit myself. I must learn how the world works. I want to know about nature and science. I want to build machines and also make art.

1482
Florence, Italy

The Duke of Milan has asked me to make a statue for him. I want to make a large horse. The horse will be 8 feet tall (2.4 m), the same height as in real life. Many sculptors have tried to make a large bronze standing horse. No one has succeeded. Even my teacher, Verrocchio, failed.

My horse will display my talent. I will make the most beautiful horse in history! I leave soon for Milan.

1484
Milan, Italy

The Duke has grand plans for my statue. Now he wants it to be much larger!

I cannot make progress on my horse. The Duke wants me to do too many projects. He wants me to write music. He asks me to plan buildings and canals. He wants me to write poems! Perhaps things were better in Verrocchio's workshop.

1498
Milan, Italy

Finally, the clay model is done. It is 24 feet (7.3 m) tall. I am pleased with it. Each day I draw and write in my notebook. I search for a way to cast the horse in bronze.

1499
Milan, Italy

The French army has come to Milan. My clay horse was standing in a field. The model was a perfect target. The soldiers aimed. They shot their arrows again and again. The horse is ruined. I have wasted many years. Today is a sad day for me.

1519
France

I am an old man now. I will never complete my beautiful bronze horse. This is my life's greatest disappointment.

From the Diary of Charlie Dent
1977
Pennsylvania

I have retired from my job as an airplane pilot. Now I hope to do some other things that I love.

I admire Leonardo da Vinci. He is a fine model for me. He had such imagination! Like Leonardo, I want to do many things. I want to express myself through art. I want to make sculptures and paint. I want to collect the work of many artists. These things will keep me busy for many years.

1978
Pennsylvania

I read an interesting article today. It told about Leonardo da Vinci. He tried to build a statue for the Duke of Milan. Leonardo worked on the statue for seventeen years. French soldiers ruined the statue. Leonardo never finished it.

I will finish Leonardo's horse. Then I will give the horse to the people of Italy. The horse will represent friendship between America and Italy.

1981

I will build a glass dome as a workshop. Then people can see the model horse.

Charlie Dent with model of bronze horse

1992

I have made more than twenty-five models in wax and clay. Finally, my model horse is complete.

1994

The doctors gave me bad news today. I will not live long enough to see the bronze horse. I do not care whether I have my name on the horse. Many people have helped me on this project. I hope they will finish it someday.

From the Diary of the Sculptor Nina Akamu

1996

I have a new project. Charlie Dent began the statue of a horse. I will try to complete the statue.

I must learn everything about Leonardo's original plan. Exactly what did Leonardo have in mind? We will never know. I can only make guesses based on his drawings. I hope that my statue looks like the horse he imagined.

Leonardo's teacher, Verrocchio, was my favorite painter. This project will connect me to the finest artists in history.

1998

I could not fix Charlie Dent's model. The model resisted the changes I tried to make. We have decided to start over.

I spoke to many scholars. They studied Leonardo's writings and his drawings. They shared ideas about how to build the horse. I began a new design.

First, I will make a new eight-foot (2.4 m) clay model. Many people will help make the model larger. Then the statue will be cast in bronze. The full-size statue will be 24 feet (7.3 m) tall. It will have the same proportions as my small model. Leonardo and Charlie wanted a grand horse. I think they would be pleased.

From the Homework of an Italian Child
2001 Milan, Italy

Today my class went to a park in Milan. We saw a huge statue of a horse. It was strong and beautiful.

I want to become an artist and a sculptor. I want to be like Leonardo da Vinci. Also, I want to visit America some day. Then I can thank the Americans for Leonardo's horse.

Author's Note:

The entries in this book are made up. They are based on facts about Leonardo and others who helped make his dream become real.